Forbidden Fantasies:
A Guide to Sexual Role-play

or

Rites to Pleasure

by

Rocco Lordes II

{Gold Alter} Press

goldalterpress.com

Published in the United States
by Gold Alter Press
Ben "Bookbeard" Fledger, Publisher

Copyright © 2015 by Rocco Lordes II.

ISBN-13: 978-0692475492 ISBN-10: 0692475494

Forbidden Fantasies: A Guide to Sexual Role-play or Rites to Pleasure

All rights reserved. No part of this publication may be reproduced or transmitted in any form or by any means, electronic or mechanical, including photocopy, recording, or any information storage and retrieval system, without the prior written permission of the publisher.

Cover: "Das Schiff Satans" by Romana Klee is licensed under CC BY 2.0.

For my dearest one.

Contents

CONSENT DISCLAIMER 7

A PREFACE 9

RITUALS 11

    I. STRANGER IN THE NIGHT 13

    II. THE REPAIRMAN 15

    III. THE POLICEMAN & CRIMINAL 17

    IV. THE TEACHER & STUDENT 18

    V. THE KIDNAPPING 20

    VI. DADDY & DAUGHTER 22

    VII. THE MASTER & SLAVE 25

FOR FURTHER STUDY 27

Consent Disclaimer

WARNING: Fictitious, gross abuses of consent are depicted in the following guidebook. Neither the publisher, nor any of Gold Alter Press's editors promote non-consensual sexual relations. Please do not engage in sexual relations without verbalized consent.

A Preface

I awoke, and there was darkness. Moon ticks, star tocks. We labor through the abyss of everyday life. Only in dreams we meet the light. Secrets presented to me in youth yielded ripe fruit. Revelation is opening. This work is a gateway.

You are owed more. Boredom is the devil's toothache. Take more. Why hesitate? The phantom of future conscience? A feeble old man, your last remaining sentinel? Already your pen trembles over the deed. I smell your ink dribbling on the page—exquisite honey. Creation too precious to lie fallow until death.

If you are content with God's table scraps, starve eternally. If it is known to you that aching appetites can be filled by the ample cup of a different world, seek me.

Say Yes now three times aloud. Once with your left eye closed. Then once in darkness. And at last open—

Rituals I–VII

STRANGER IN THE NIGHT

Implements: A bar, Money, Alcohol.

Believe in magic. Amid the gray sea of faces at the bar, there, alone, you see The Stranger. His gaze catches you; a simple spell. How else explain the struggle to break from his flashing eyes? Resume banter with your ugly friends. You think only of him. His hands pawing at your hips, breasts. Pawing you beneath him. This desire to penetrate, to feed—a need to open awakened. Wander from your safety. Go to him. Words, a drink, a dark ride; blur. Both participants want one thing. And all that is required is to loose a dark corner of your soul to The Stranger in the Night.

To initiate The Stranger in the Night with a partner, you must leave the comfort of home. You deserve this. Any place where fun with others is to be had will suffice. Lose your partner. Mingle. See your partner with the others. Let them see you. Pacify concerns with drink. Dance and increase energy. Listen to your body. It guides the way. The past?—tired tune. The future? PATIENCE: This sole scene will not cure all. Drink at the river; forget. Laugh when your desire is peaked sharp enough to murder.

Catch your mate and tear them away. Words are meaningless. Will you make the tiny sacrifice? It must be done at once: A bathroom stall. A backseat. A roadside motel. Speak only in directives during the encounter. Do not speak of anything that relates to this other, The Stranger. Even words of desire. Speak with your bodies. During the ritual, see your partner as they were with others before you, and how they could be with others after or during you, independent of your will. They are a silhouette of a person, fucking to fuck. You are of no consequence. Neither do they matter. They too see you in this new light—faceless conqueror. Stare through new eyes upon the body of the demon whose bed you share, whose dark hair your fingers grasp.

Understand this: Each initiate exists only as a vehicle. Where are we going? A state of pleasure refined. Already you have considered and know this to be true. You are not touching to extinguish your desire—a quick screw. At the root of this ritual is the manifestation of an impersonal pleasure: to enjoy each other as: chalice & mouth, alter & dagger, creation & god, etc.

This gateway scenario frees pleasure into an entity separable from the identity or will of each participant. Such pleasure does not discriminate only in so far as others are of service to it. It seeks to be, free and indomitable; what any being wants.

The Stranger should leave soon after. Again, speak little and no meddling words. No false platitudes feigning union. For at least an hour remain separate. Void is necessary. Always there, only now its tugging gravity. Saturn, swallowing his children whole. How to deal with such masterful force? Sacrifice to appease.

Your loving partner returns with coffee or a favorite dessert. Kiss and return to your daily routine and identities. Masks are a comfort. Beneath, your encounter remains untouchable. Carry it proudly inside of you. His crystal seed, most sacrosanct. Exquisite and terrible secret.

The Repairman

Implements: Tools, Alcohol.

It's a little nothing. You have an itch. He can fix it. The Repairman! A small fee? It's nothing. Your husband needs never to know. All deserve this. And to see it—the surface of a spot well scratched. Tip of his hat! Call anytime.

The Repairman is a simple ritual to continue the opening. The Repairman appears at your doorstep to fix an agreed upon, non-sexual task within your dwelling with the understanding that if completed adequately, there are other tasks around the home that will need doing. All exchanges should be conducted formally with the titles Mr., Mrs., Miss., appropriately. Conversation while checking in on The Repairman should remain on the task at hand. Bring him a strong alcoholic beverage: "You must be thirsty." Undergarments or parts of the body may be revealed that betray a working relationship.

During the length of the work, be in the nearest possible room pleasuring yourself. Fantasize until you decide upon one distinct act that must be performed to satisfy the desire you bear. As you are called to check in with The Repairman, no details should be revealed verbally about the mischief you are conjuring. An increasingly disheveled look will subliminally hint at it. Among other deviances: Wet your hand with your sex, then offer a hand. Slip any object you bring to The Repairman first into your genitals. Sip from his drink so that his mouth will meet yours at that spot. This is an old form of witchcraft that works adequately.

When the non-sex task is performed to your satisfaction, The Repairman will ask, "Is there anything else that I can fix for you, Mrs. _____?" At this point, call him to where you await or put the task before him. Endless pleasure isn't a laughing matter—do not smile or laugh. Your relationship to The Repairman remains impersonal:

"Yes—I need you to lick my pussy to climax. I've been trying to orgasm for one half hour with no results and that would be a help."

Remember: What you are asking for is a job that needs work performed on it. The importance of its success lies above what you want and even The Repairman. Never forget this.

"Any better now?" he may ask during the job. "A little more on the left," you estimate, as if hanging curtains.

And after? Formality is maintained:

"Great—that does it," you say.

"Glad to be of service," he replies, packing his fish tape. "If it gives you trouble again, ma'am, call anytime."

"I'll do that."

This exchange is imperative and should deviate little from the script.

This liminal ritual allows pleasure to take on form. Now it stretches, making limbs.

Rejoice! You're birthing a glory.

The Policeman & Criminal

Implements: Handcuffs, Baton, Leather gloves, Rip-able attire.

You were only combing your hair in the mirror before being thrown and shouted at:

"Get on the ground! Now! Now!!! Put your arms behind your back! Open your mouth—take this! No—deeper!"

You wriggle, claw, resist arrest. Exact vengeance upon your partner in the form of psychosexual violence. A struggle! Who will be The Master?

Such is the fun of The Policeman & Criminal.

The Policeman & Criminal begins when a sex act is agreed upon at least three days beforehand. A Criminal is thus aware that in only a matter of time they will be subjected to an exact punishment. The reaping only occurs when a Criminal is unaware. They can never ask for it. Once pursuit is initiated, the act moves forward to conclusion no matter what state a Criminal is in. The Policeman must follow the law.

A Criminal does not submit to The Policeman. The Policeman is but a public servant of the law of desire. Always desire is to be obeyed. Do not resist the law. Resist being the sacrifice and not the red robed priest that rises above. But desire demands both roles filled, and to this law both must inevitably submit.

This transversal ritual completes the extrication of pleasure outside will. It stalks on its six legs within you, demanding to be fulfilled. The vaginal/anal/oral passages are entrances to it. Opening invites further revelation.

The Teacher & Student

Implements: Desk and chairs set, Appropriate attire (formal dress for The Teacher and uniform for Student).

A Student sits penitent beside your desk. "I've done all the work you've asked," she says, "and I don't have a passing grade."

"You must emulate the behavior of your peers."

"I am, sir. Still you return me poor grades. I don't know what it is I am doing wrong."

"You do not listen to me."

"I can't fail anymore. My parents will kill me. I will do anything to pass."

"You will do anything?"

"Yes, sir."

"Then, now, do exactly as I say."

For a Student, pleasure during this gateway ritual is fed from her risk, vulnerability, and abandonment of conventional values. For The Teacher, pleasure is fed from his command, disregard for the conventional worth of his subject, and the introduction of a new system of order. For this reason, it is imperative at the end that The Teacher approves of a Student's performance in a manner that is assertive, evaluative, and begs gratitude, which a Student must then supply in earnest.

The crux of The Teacher & Student scenario rests upon a Student needing desperately some non-sex related mark/evaluation/approval from The Teacher that is solely under his discretion and power. This scenario can as well be played under the boss/employee guise. Any social transgression will work in which one petitions another on a higher ledge of power. These exchanges denigrate the person of lesser power because one's identity in terms of skills and knowledge and ability (all that one misbelieves is important in status elevation) become irrelevant. The previously ignored sex value of a Student becomes all-important: One is evaluated only in terms of sex capital, a curio at the least. Exquisite pleasure rears its head when a student crosses this threshold, assenting to relinquish identity in the great service of desire.

A Student is henceforth at the will of The Teacher's exercise of power. Perform positions that exaggerate the subordinate/superior dynamic: oral sex (The Teacher standing, Student kneeling), face down with rear up, various (Student) prone positions. The Teacher should stay mostly dressed, while a Student is progressively stripped down to garments she would be embarrassed to be seen in by her peers and family.

Throughout the scene, it should be clear that a Student is being pressured into performing for The Teacher who is ever evaluating:

"That's good. No—arch your back—better."

Some negotiation on the part of a Student is encouraged to remind both participants of their transgression:

"I don't think I can."

"Do you want the good grade?"

Though the roles of The Teacher & Student are mere constructs, using convention in this gateway ritual lends form and structure to the chaos of desire. Incarnations of pleasure may be boundless, but form allows pleasure to refine, deepen, and mature.

The Kidnapping

Implements: Rope, Blindfold, Ball gag, Lubricant, Misc. devices.

A woman finds herself helpless: tied up, alone, unable to call for help—and at the whims of a madman who will stop at nothing to satiate his lust.

The Kidnapper does what he wishes—her choice in the matter has been extricated. He performs in silence upon her, but for the occasional slip of hot breath during his work of removing or tearing clothing, not wanting to reveal the sound of his voice, any clue that might identify him after the act ... if he so chooses to let her live!

A simple way to induce the anxiety necessary for The Kidnapping to be successful is to disorient a victim. If performing in a location that a victim is familiar with, blackout vision with a blindfold or bag over the head and spin the female around several times. Securing headphones to a victim's head and playing music at an extreme volume can aid in this process. Push her then through the area until you are certain she is bewildered. From the blinding onward, neither participant speaks. This allows the victim's imagination to run. Who is this man on her back? What does he look like? Is he someone she has met? One of her friends? A member of the family? Victim: Allow your imagination to run the gamut during The Kidnapping.

Once disoriented, the binding of limbs begins. Restriction in terms of range of motion and ability is required. Every sense and ability removed by The Kidnapper puts that power under his control. Threats and rough handling of a victim are encouraged. Such performance aims to induce fear, not pain. Pain is only used when needed to induce fear. The proportion of pleasure garnered is proportional to the resulting amount of fear for both The Kidnapper and his victim.

Because force is required, lubricant can be necessary. Penetration of yet resisting orifices without lubricant may unpleasantly damage the sex organs of both participants. However, as The Kidnapping actualizes your partner's fantasies of rape, often her genitals are made uncontrollably wet from the scene itself. Discuss the details of her particular fantasies and, if such details fuel you, work them into the ritual.

During this liminal ritual, The Kidnapper is a servant of pleasure, nothing more. The dark knife of pleasure demands; he strikes. To a Victim in this scene, The Kidnapper is no longer a servant of pleasure—pleasure itself works upon her! Picking clean your bones of every made-available delight, you sacred animal, alter of Set, chalice of the magic blood. Here, the willful desire of each participant assumes form to serve the greater god.

Daddy & Daughter

Implements: A darkened bedroom, Youthful attire (for Baby), Red robe (for Daddy).

Baby is growing up. Upon her innocent thoughts of ponies and rainbows and tea parties with Dolly, paralyzing clouds of lust encroach. It began after distinguishing the outline of Daddy's semi-hard member in his undershorts one night. Her panties moistened at the thought. Rubbing the spot made her feel close to Daddy. Soon daughter wishes to do the unspeakable, if only one time, with the man she worships. The pressure becomes too much for her to subdue with idle masturbation. A servant of desire, our most precious imp creeps into Daddy's room at midnight to tempt her father into the ultimate transgression....

The Daddy & Daughter ritual involves advances that negotiate intense physical desire against social conventions that dictate that a sex act between them is wrong, perhaps immoral. What starts as an encounter to satiate physical curiosity—lust overcoming social convention—ultimately falls back upon the convention (the ever-present rule of patriarchy in the familial unit) to achieve maximum pleasure.

From most casual incest erotica to Nabokov's literary masterpiece, "Lolita," Daddy & Daughter encounters are always initiated by Baby. She must coax Daddy's desire for (what she mistakenly believes will be) a no-strings-attached romp with fresh and eager meat. The goal is to force his desire to trump his obligations to protect his charge from evil. This can be achieved by pushing normal bounds of physical contact typically maintained by a father and daughter. She will write off such advances as NBD (no big deal). With each catlike stretch and stroke, she invites Daddy to be intoxicated by the scent of the sex conquest of someone he intrinsically cares for and aims to protect. Naturally Daddy finds himself physically aroused, at first ashamed at his failure to uphold standards of decency. But Baby rubs against him, purrs, begging to be pet.

"Don't you think I'm pretty, Daddy?"

"You're gorgeous, Baby."

"Don't you think I'm sexy?"

"You are, but—"

Power exchange happens at this point.

"I'm yours, daddy. You can take what's yours."

Once overcome, Daddy leads. Daddy typically pushes the boundaries initially set by Baby. Baby may have talked him into feeling her breasts, looking at her privates, or allowing her to touch his manhood. Once incensed, Daddy cajoles for more, using her initial logic to force the point when she hesitates:

"I don't know, Daddy."

His response: "But don't you want to please your daddy? Don't you want to be daddy's girl?"

Whatever she does beyond this point, Baby does reluctantly, as if fearing pain, or now, consequences. Here we hear, "Ow, Daddy, it hurts," when pleasure is most intense.

Daddy again uses the logic twisted to his advantage: "If you want to please your daddy, let me do X for a little longer."

Her consent is absolutely necessary: "Yes, Daddy."

If pushed further and Baby's resistance is again encountered, the following exchange must occur:

"Aren't you my good little girl?"

"Yes, Daddy."

"Don't you want to make him feel good?"

"Yes, I'm yours. My pussy is yours, too."

"I'm going to do X then."

"It's all yours, Daddy. Do what you wish."

"That's my good girl."

The point where total power is given to Daddy is the climax of this ritual.

Orgasm for both ends in Baby underscoring the act being committed: "Yes, Daddy, fuck your little girl!"

Returning later to the scenario in a narrative fashion (X happened last time, and now...) relies upon Baby being initially resistant to give up herself again to Daddy ("My Y really hurt after last time." "But didn't Z feel good?" "Yes, Daddy."), assenting to his authority, and taking pleasure in sexually pleasing Daddy in ways that only she can/is willing to.

This transversal ritual defines each participant's role in the service of desire. The work must be done to secure His ever-lasting glory.

The Master & Slave

Implements: All. Or none.

"Hold open your pussy," says The Master

Slave does so with one hand.

"Not with the one hand—with two, like I taught you. Do you listen to me?" He smacks Slave in the head.

"I'm sorry, sir. I will do better next time, sir."

"You will after this punishment. Remember the rules? Each time you don't listen, I fuck your ass as hard as I want for thirty seconds."

"Yes, sir." Slave holds open her ass with two hands.

"See? You're learning already...."

Do not confuse The Master & Slave ritual with another. Between Daddy & Daughter, power is given incrementally and complete at climax, nor does it model an antagonist as in The Kidnapping. With The Master & Slave total power exchange is a given. The fun lies in a Slave never being able to meet the strict demands of The Master. At first, it is perhaps best to agree upon major acts beforehand. How a Slave performs those acts become subject of The Master's scrutiny, discipline, and punishment. His work is to direct a Slave to display a correct behavior or inflict upon her acts of pain, degradation, and/or humiliation.

Together, The Master & Slave manifest pleasure's highest sacrifice—total domination of a human subject until a Slave's only desire is to serve The Master. Rightly, each will be rewarded with visions beyond the limits and known only to the faithful. The obsidian rule: Absolute subservience renders pleasure absolute.

There is one greater service: Slaves that make Slaves, teaching right behavior so they too can serve The Master. What a glorious day it will be when all mothers and daughters and their children so on are bent into exemplars of the work!

Go, now, believers. Gleaming sickles baptized with virgin tears! Handsome cannibals stalking the statuary of dark gods! Living stones of Red Mountain. The devoted. The damned.

For Further Study

Georges Bataille "story of the eye"

"atlas shrugged" Ayn Rand

"Beyond Good and Evil" Friedrich Nietzsche

"Rosemary's Baby" Roman Polanski

"inland Empire" david Lynch

"The Book of Lies" Aleister Crowley

"The erotic Poems" Ovid

Marquis de sade "Justine"

"Mysteries of the unknown" Time-Life

"Lolita" Vladamir nabokov

~~"dreaming the Dark" Starhawk~~

"The Satanic Bible" anton Szandor LaVey

"A Vision" W. B. yeats

"The Book of Abramelin" Abraham von Worms

Carole maso "aureole"

"song of solomon" The Bible

"Led Zeppelin IV" Led Zeppelin

www.ingramcontent.com/pod-product-compliance
Lightning Source LLC
LaVergne TN
LVHW051808080426
835511LV00019B/3441